WALKING CLOSE ˙

and the DEEPINGS

Number Twenty Nine in the popular series of walking guides

<u>Contents</u>

Walked, Written and Drawn by Clive Brown
Clive Brown © 2004 – 2012

Published by Clive Brown
ISBN 978-1-907669-29-3

PLEASE
Take care of the countryside
Your leisure is someone's livelihood

Close gates
Start no fires
Keep away from livestock and animals
Do not stray from marked paths
Take litter home
Do not damage walls, hedgerows or fences
Cross only at stiles or gates
Protect plants, trees and wildlife
Keep dogs on leads
Respect crops, machinery and rural property
Do not contaminate water

Although not essential we recommend good walking boots; during hot weather take something to drink on the way. All walks can easily be negotiated by an averagely fit person. The routes have been recently walked and surveyed, changes can however occur, please follow any signed diversions. Some paths cross fields which are under cultivation. All distances and times are approximate.

The maps give an accurate portrayal of the area, but scale has however been sacrificed in some cases for the sake of clarity and to fit restrictions of page size.

Walking Close To have taken every care in the research and production of this guide but cannot be held responsible for the safety of anyone using them.

During very wet weather, parts of these walks may become impassable through flooding, check before starting out. Stiles and rights of way can get overgrown during the summer; folding secateurs are a useful addition to a walker's rucksack.

Thanks to Angela for help in production of these booklets

Views or comments?
walkingcloseto@yahoo.co.uk

29:D

Walking Close to Bourne
and the Deepings

Bourne is placed in south Lincolnshire, right on the edge of the fens with low undulating hills to the west, while to the east flat fenland stretches away into the distance. This selection of routes makes use of paths, bridleways, rights of way and national recreational paths in the countryside close to Bourne and Market Deeping. There is very little walking on roads except where unavoidable. Most are on firm, good quality paths and well marked and signposted. Paths may cross fields under cultivation and some are more obscure and less well directed; the detailed instructions will guide past these points. Some of the walks are in areas popular with walkers already; others are in areas less popular and perhaps less accessible.

Grimsthorpe Castle has been owned by the de Eresby family since it was given by Henry VIII to the 10th Baron as a wedding gift to celebrate his marriage to Maria de Salinas, a kinswoman and lady in waiting to Katherine of Aragon. The impressive north front was built by Vanbrugh in the early 18th century; the park and gardens were laid out by Capability Brown in 1771.

The town is the reputed birthplace in around 1032 of the Saxon folk hero Hereward the Wake. He became disaffected with the new regime about 4 years after the 1066 Norman Invasion and joined forces with other rebels and some locally based Danes. They sacked Peterborough Abbey, set up a fort in the easily defended Isle of Ely and created havoc throughout the Fenland area. King William however made a separate peace with the Danes who left Hereward carrying on a guerrilla campaign with a few followers. After a siege the remaining outlaws surrendered, Hereward disappeared, dropping out of history and into folklore.

Bourne is also the birthplace of William Cecil and Charles Worth. Cecil (1520-1598), who became Lord Burghley in 1571, was born in the house in the town centre which is now the Burghley Arms Hotel. After running England's affairs for a number of years as the chief minister of Elizabeth I he retired to Burghley House, the grand stately home he had built near Stamford. Charles Worth (1825-1895) was born in a house on North Street now marked by a plaque. He founded the House of Worth one of the first and most influential 19th century Paris couturiers.

We feel that it would be difficult to get lost with the instructions and map in this booklet, but recommend carrying an Ordnance Survey map. All walks are on Explorer maps Nos. 235, 247 and 248; Landranger Nos. 130 & 142 cover at a smaller scale. Roads, geographical features and buildings, not on our map but visible from the walk, can be easily identified.

1   Hacconby Spinney

5^1/$_4$ Miles   2^1/$_2$ Hours

Find a Parking space in Morton, pubs and shops in village. No toilets. Start from the church. **May be muddy in wet weather.**

1   Cross the road to the Church Hall, turn right and walk 70yds to the footpath sign. Turn left down the gravel and tarmac drive, go over the stile and turn right. Pass through the kissing gate and take the arrowed direction straight on over two more stiles and go along the road ahead to the A15; cross this busy road carefully.

2   Carry on straight ahead on the path between nos 14 & 16. Maintain direction over the stile, the hedged paths, the field at the back of the houses and the line of trees on the field edge leading eventually to a stile in a hedge line. Step over the stile and take a slight left across the field beyond, which may be under cultivation although a path should be well marked within any crop, to a signpost. Turn right along the farm track this side of the hedge and walk up to the road.

3   Turn left to the T-junction and right along to the green triangle. At the signpost on the left, turn left along the narrow path between the fence and the hedge, turn left with the fence still left and take the track right, along the right hand field edge with the hedge to the right. Continue as the hedge stops on the field edge with the dyke now to the right and follow it to the footbridge.

4   Cross and go up the short left hand field edge, turn left and follow the field edge through a boundary to the four way signpost. Turn right with the dyke to the left, as the dyke ends cross to the corner of the fence and continue the original direction with the fence now right. Go under the barbed wire in the corner and take a left hand diagonal over this field, crossing a footbridge halfway; a track should be well marked within any crop. Continue direction under the overhead wires and cross the stile onto the road.

5   Take the road to the right into Stainfield, at the T-junction turn right and follow the road to the signpost on the left. Turn left along the left hand field edge and follow the track around a double bend to the boundary. Turn left on a farm track and immediate right with the dyke to the right, as the dyke bears right go straight on over the open field (a track should be visible). Keep going on the left hand field edge up to the lay-by.

6   Bear right, around tiny Hacconby Spinney, over the A15 and across the stile in the hedge gap on the other side. Carry on over this field parallel to the right hand side. Cross the stile/footbridge at the far end and keep direction on the left field edges up to the road. Continue direction towards Haconby village, after 120yds, at the signpost, turn right over the double stile.

7 Go over the field and the footbridge ahead, carry on along the edge of the sports field and go over the footbridge in the easily missed hedge gap. A track should be visible in this field on a

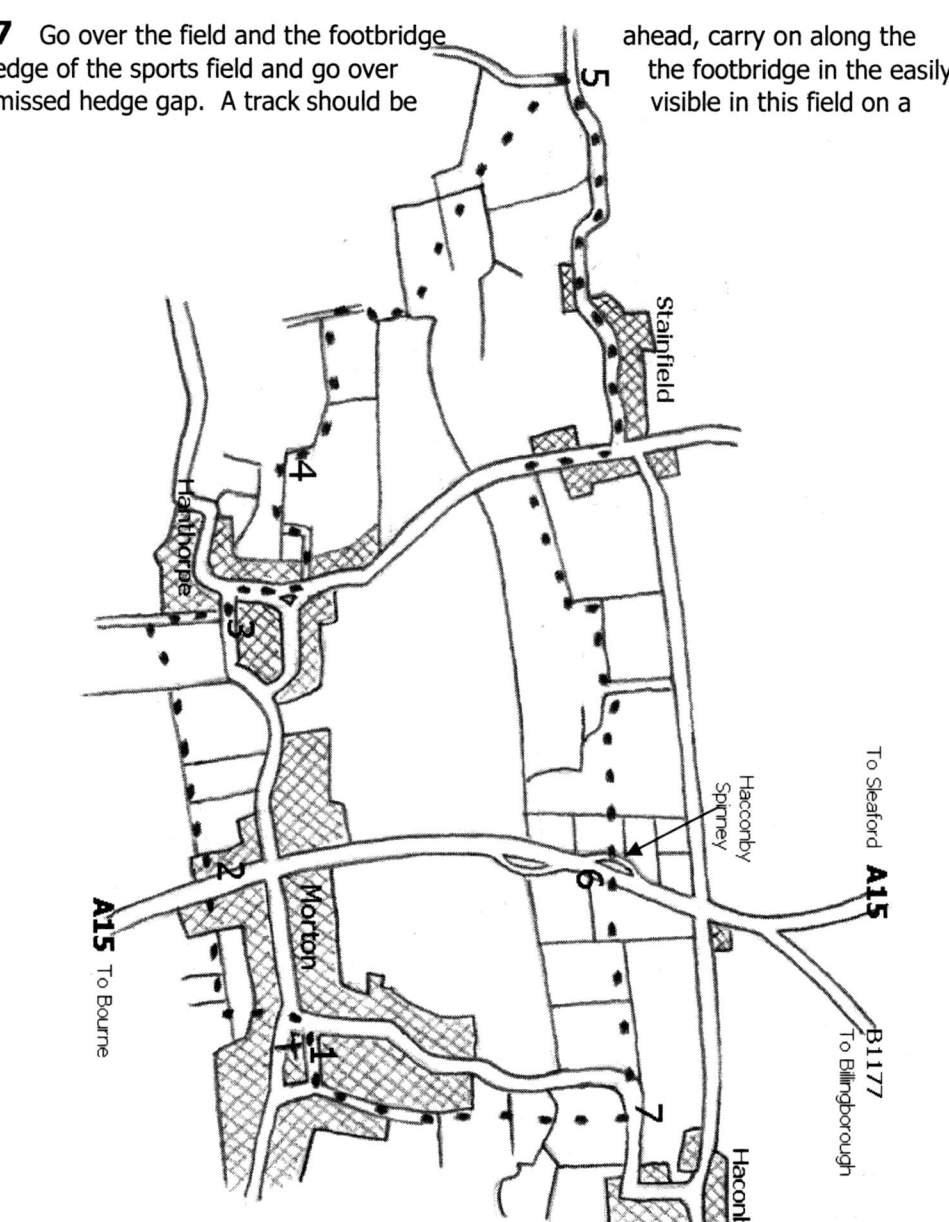

slight right hand diagonal forking left to the left hand corner of the tall hedge at the back of the houses. Continue direction behind the houses, at the hedge end marker post bear left to the top corner. Turn right along the farm road which leads into Morton and your vehicle.

29:D

2   Maxey Watermill

5^1/$_2$ Miles   2^1/$_2$ Hours

Park in the centre of Market Deeping or the shopping centre car park off Godsey Lane. Toilets, cafes, pubs, shops and takeaways all close.

1   Start from the town centre; go along Bridge Foot towards Peterborough, cross to the right hand side of the road and walk over the bridge. At the footpath sign turn right over the stile, double back with the bridge to the right and bear left on the riverside path. Bear left then right keeping the river loop to the right and carry on to the A15 Deepings By-pass.

2   Continue under the bridge and follow the track back to the main river; follow the riverbank as it forks left. After nearly three quarters of a mile bear left away from the main river along a field edge with a tree lined often dry watercourse to the right. Cross the footbridge onto the road and turn right.

3   At Maxey Watermill turn right at the signpost over the stile down the side of the building and turn left along the grass with the mill house to the left. Continue under the pipeline and bear right over a stile just before a gate, walk down the right hand field edge, trees, hedge and stream to the right. Cross the footbridge/stile and bear right along the long field, passing close to the corner on the left, up to the stile right of the white gate and turn right along the road.

4   Continue over the bridge into West Deeping village and turn right into The Lane. Go past the brick gateposts into the courtyard of new houses and turn left at the footpath sign on the low fence. Bear right between the fence and the wall behind the house to the signpost; carry on along the farm track with the wide dyke to the right. The path eventually reaches a wire fence; turn left on the path between the fence and the hedge all the way to the A16.

5   Cross this busy road and turn right on the roadside path, go across the bridge over the drain and turn left over the gate at the footpath sign. Take a right hand diagonal over the field and the stile in the hedge; keep direction over the next field which may be under cultivation although a track should be well marked within any crop. Bear right at the corner and walk up to the Deepings by-pass.

6   This is again a very busy road, cross with care and maintain direction through the gap and across the field to Millfield Road. Turn right and immediate left up the narrow enclosed path to Tattershall Drive. Turn right, walk up to Stamford Road and follow it left back into the centre of Market Deeping and your vehicle.

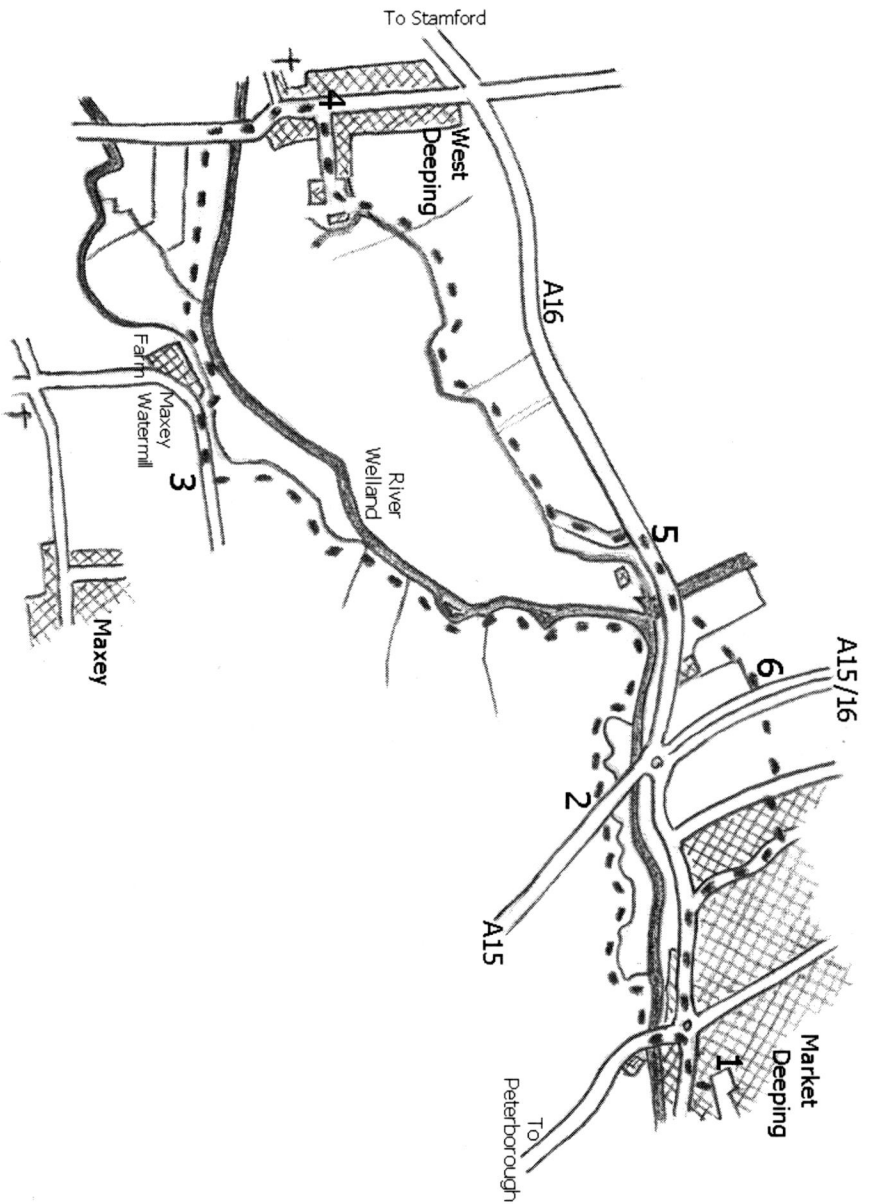

3 Addah Wood

$6^1/_2$ Miles   3 to $3^1/_2$ Hours

Find a parking space in Castle Bytham, no toilets, local shop and pubs the 'Castle Inn' and the 'Fox and Hounds Inn'. **Will be muddy in wet weather.**

1 Head out of the village north west towards South Witham, turn left over the stile opposite Water Lane. Cross the field to the bottom of the embankment, this and other fields on this walk may be under cultivation but tracks should be visible within any crops. Turn right through the boundary and up the slope on the left hand field edge, cross the stile to the left and go through the tunnel under the disused railway.

2 Cross the stile at the end and take a right hand diagonal over the field (a track should be visible); go through the gap at the boundary and carry on along left hand field edges with the dyke to the left. Continue parallel to Little Haw Wood up to a stile and turn left, over the footbridge. Carry on up the slope, turn right and go around the corner of the trees.

3 Walk along the side of the wood with the wire fence to the left. In the corner go straight on through the gateway and keep direction through the trees on a fairly indistinct path marked by an occasional white top post. Carry on to the yellow top post marked with a blue disc and turn right.

4 Go past the next marker post close to the walls of Stocken Prison. Turn left for 30yds and then right, back to the original direction. Continue in Addah Wood parallel to the prison, veer left with the path and carry on along the left hand field edge with the trees still on the left. Bear left through a gap in the hedge at a marker post and immediate right on the right hand field edge.

5 As this edge swings right, take a diagonal left over the field to a marked gap; maintain direction over the next field and down the farm track with the hedge and trees to the left. Bear left with the track and take an immediate right through a narrow gate. Walk down the path between the trees and exit through another narrow gate.

6 Bear right on the hardcore farm track and continue into Clipsham. Turn left at the junction along the road between stone walls; bear right to the main road and then left along the roadside path. At the road junction with the signpost go straight on through the gate across the open field, past the tree to a yellow top post.

7 Keep direction on left hand field edges and the hardcore road. Close to the farm bear right through metal gates, turn left through the next set of gates, up the tree lined roadway. Turn left at the signpost close to the rear of a house.

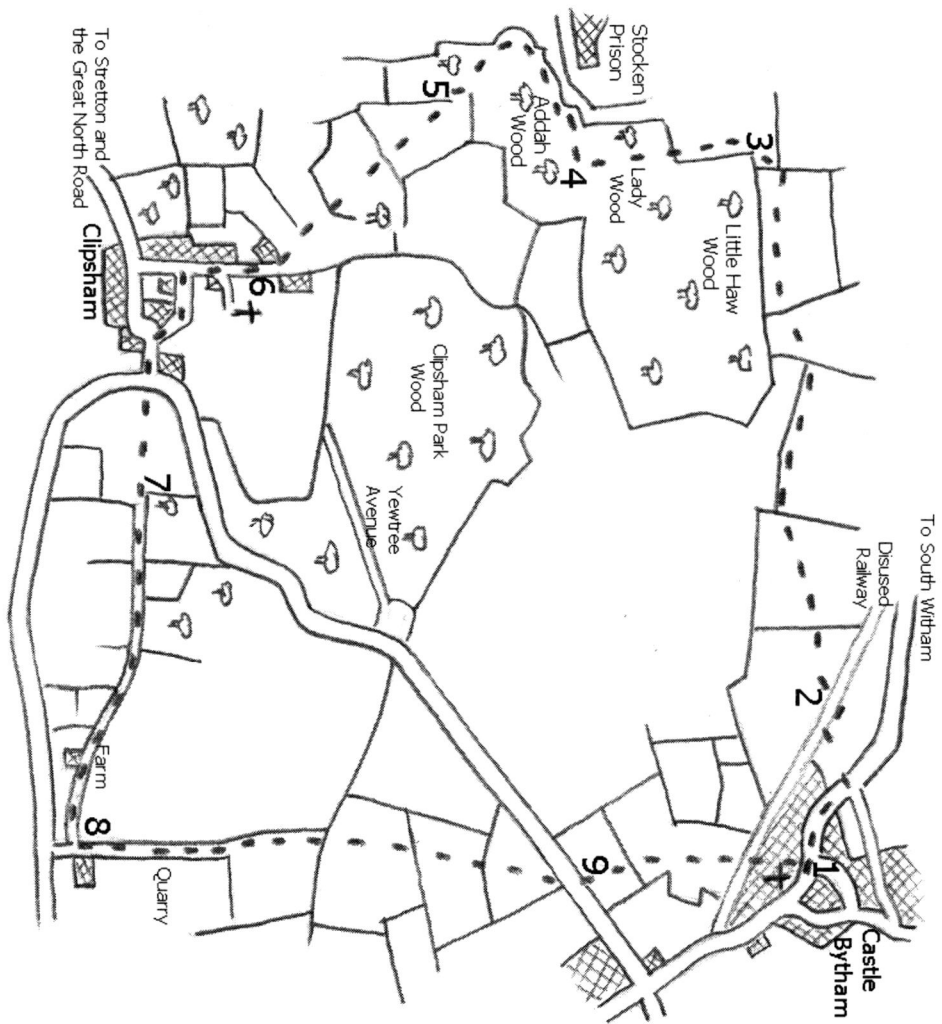

8   Follow this narrow path between trees and bushes, with the quarry lower down to the right, all the way to a stile/footbridge. Cross, go past a fenced plantation of young trees and over another footbridge/stile. Keep direction over the next three fields all of which should have paths visible within any crops up to the road at the top field corner.

9   Cross the road and maintain direction over the large field beyond (track should be clear) to the signpost in the hedge ahead. Go over the old railway bridge, bear left then right next to the cemetery, turn left at the corner and follow the path down the slope past the church and into the village to find your vehicle.

4   Car Dyke

5¹/₂ Miles   2³/₄ Hours

Park in Bourne, several car parks, toilets, pubs, shops, cafes and takeaways. Start from the market place/town centre.

1   Go along Spalding Road for nearly half a mile up to Eastgate and turn right, continue straight on over the bridge down Willoughby Road. Just after Burmor Close turn right at the signpost along the path with Car Dyke to the right.

2   Follow the path left, go across the road and carry on along the left hand bank for a mile and a quarter to the road.

3   Keep direction on this left hand bank for another half a mile, past the farm buildings on the opposite bank to a footbridge and cross, turning left to get back to the original direction on the other bank. Go over a narrow tarmac road and the stile, walk up to the stile at the top left, do not cross, turn right up the left hand field edge, step over the stile and go through the enclosed path to the A15.

4   Cross this busy road with care and turn right along the roadside path to the signpost. Turn left through the wide gateway, follow the field edge right then left over a footbridge in the corner; keep direction to a signpost and turn right along the track. At the farmyard turn right then left around the barn to the road and turn left.

5   After 300yds turn right at a signpost, go across the lawn next to the bungalow and through the kissing gate. Maintain direction over this field on a path which should be clearly marked within any crop and ahead on the right hand field edge. Cross a footbridge and follow the field edge round the corner to regain direction along the edge of Math Wood. At the far corner of the wood cross the footbridge and turn right. Go over the dyke and turn left with the dyke to the left up to the signpost.

6   Turn right on the wide bridleway, keep direction over the new road and continue between barbed wire and mesh fences. Cross the hardcore road past the signpost and down the track through the trees. Turn right at an easily missed overgrown marker post along an obvious track, bear right at a junction and walk up to the houses. Turn right then left onto the estate road and follow it to the A15, turn left and walk along the roadside path back into the town centre to find your vehicle.

29:D

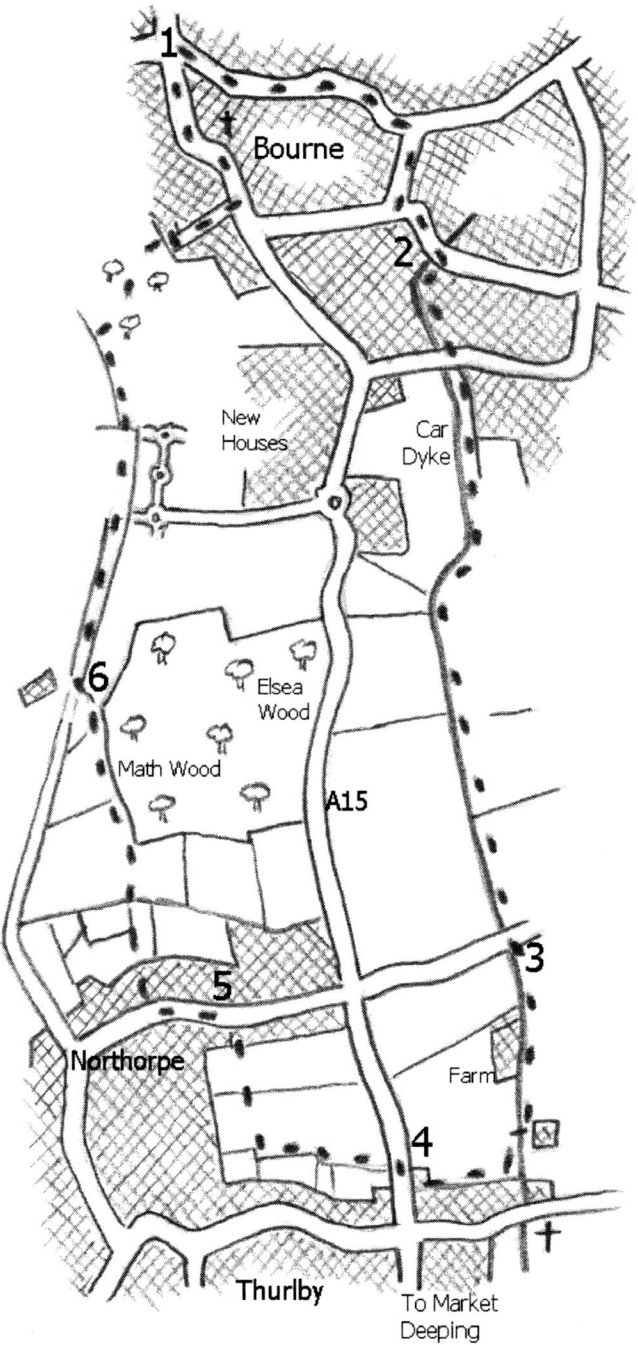

1

Bourne

2

New
Houses

Car
Dyke

6

Elsea
Wood

Math Wood

A15

5

3

Northorpe

Farm

4

Thurlby

To Market
Deeping

5 Thunderbolt Pit

$7^3/_4$ Miles $3^3/_4$ Hours

Park in the lay-by on the corner
south of Creeton (B1176).
No toilets. No facilities.

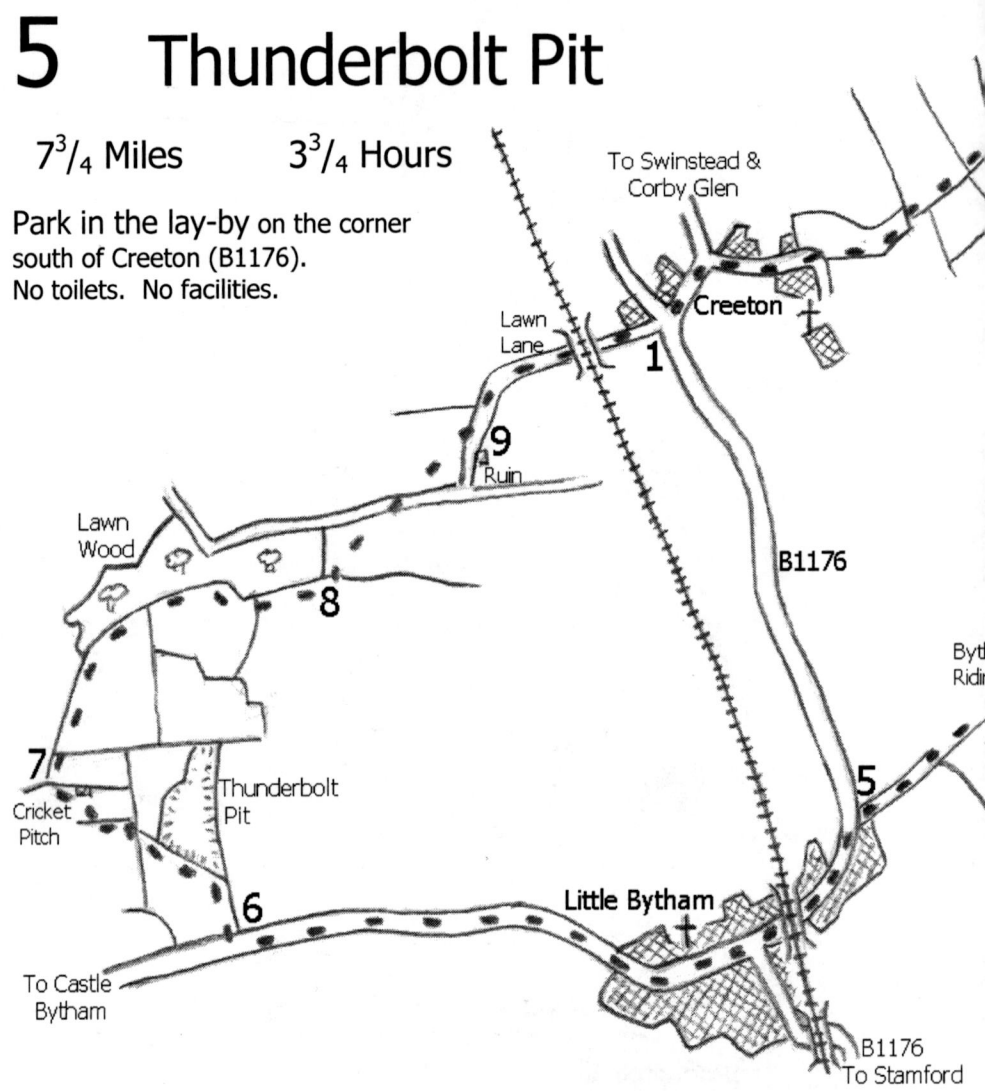

1 Bear right back into Creeton, cross the bridge and bear right. As the road turns right go straight on past the signpost and along the right hand field edge. Continue through the gate and two more fields bearing right at the end through a tall wooden gate in the corner. Keep direction through the mistletoe clad avenue of trees.

2 Cross the tarmac Chestnut Avenue and carry on out of the trees through the high gate with substantial wooden gateposts. As the trees on the right end, turn right along to the marker post and bear left between fields to the hardcore road.

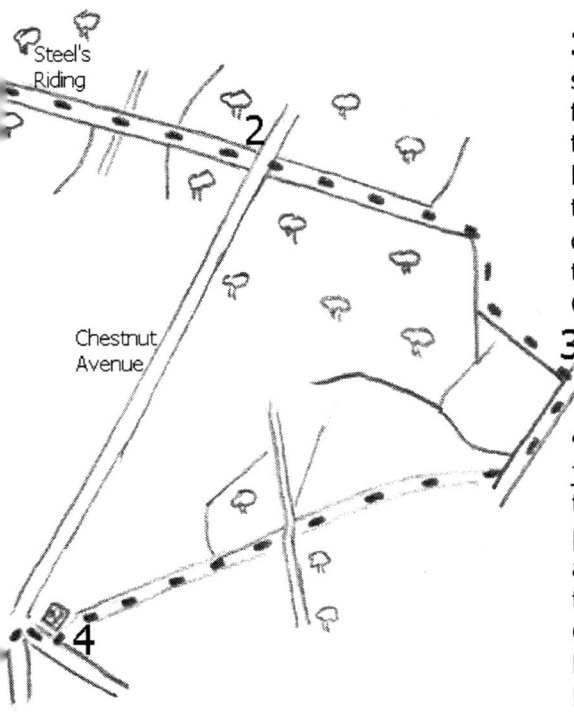

3 Turn right for 300yds to a signpost, turn right between the field and the trees and follow the track bearing left. Join the hardcore farm road, bear left through the hedge gap and keep direction between the field and the trees as the road bears left. Continue from the marker post on the grass track flanked by fields to a signpost on an estate road.

4 Turn right for 50yds to a junction next to a house, turn left then immediate right past a marker post along Bytham Riding, an avenue of chestnut trees with telegraph poles down the centre. Go through the gate and along the hedged bridleway (Park Lane) into Little Bytham.

5 At the road turn left down the roadside path, bear right under the railway bridge and follow the road out of the village for a mile and a quarter to a footpath sign.

6 Turn right along the hardcore road to the metal gate, bear left along the field edge with the hedge and Thunderbolt Pit to the right. Step over the stile and follow the line of trees on the right to a marker post, go through the gap and take a right hand diagonal to the opposite corner. Just the other side of the pavilion turn right over a stile.

7 Follow the left hand field edge up the slope, at the top bear slight right and with Lawn Wood on the left keep going to the boundary just this side of the overhead wires. Cross the dyke and turn left through the gap.

8 The path from here goes on an indistinct path diagonally over the field to a derelict brick farm building but it is often easier particularly in wet weather to walk ahead along the field edge with the trees to the left to a hardcore farm track.

9 Follow the track away from the derelict building, round the corners and through the middle arch of the railway bridge to your vehicle in the lay-by on the corner.

29:D

6   Elder Holt

7 Miles   3¹/₄ Hours

Park in Bourne Woods car park west of Bourne off the A151 near the junction with the A6121, toilets and picnic facilities.

1   Go through the gap left of the toilets and turn left along the straight path away from the playground. Continue straight on at the junction of paths, bear right and carry on for nearly half a mile to a crossroads of paths marked by a small sculpture and marker posts either side of this path.

2   Turn left and follow the grass path to the edge of the wood, cross the footbridge and continue along the left hand field edge. At the second boundary, go through the hedge gap and turn left for 50yds, *Grimsthorpe Castle can be seen in the middle distance past Edenham church.* Turn right in the corner, downhill to a marker post in the hedge gap; turn left through the gap then right to continue direction with the hedge then the dyke now on the right. Go under the wires, cross the wide concrete bridge and turn right at the signpost.

3   Walk along the field edge next to the East Glen River, a wide dyke at this point, go through the gap in the corner and turn left between the river and the trees. Turn right over the footbridge, cross the stile and turn left. Join the concrete road and follow it up to the corner at the signpost. Cross the cattle grid and turn left along the road to the A151 in Edenham.

4   Turn left, follow the roadside path and turn right into Scottlethorpe Road. Go past the houses and bear right past Tumble Row farm through Scottlethorpe, continue uphill through the gate and along the footpath on the road marked private. Cross the bridge and walk uphill with the young trees of Elder Holt to the right.

5   At the T-junction turn left and walk up to the signpost by the double gate, keep direction ahead on the right hand field edge and follow it to the left. Go through the gate in the corner and cross the field to a wooden gate in the corner at the bottom of the slope; this field may be under cultivation although a track should be visible within any crop. Bear right along the right hand field edge, look for a track in the crop and cross to the footbridge in front of the wood to the left.

6   Cross the footbridge and bear right over a stile along the field edge with the trees to the left. Keep direction when the trees end over a boundary to a footbridge and continue uphill over a stile. At the next stile bear slight left on the track along the field edge and carry on through the riding school.

Completed on the next Page (Sixteen)

29:D

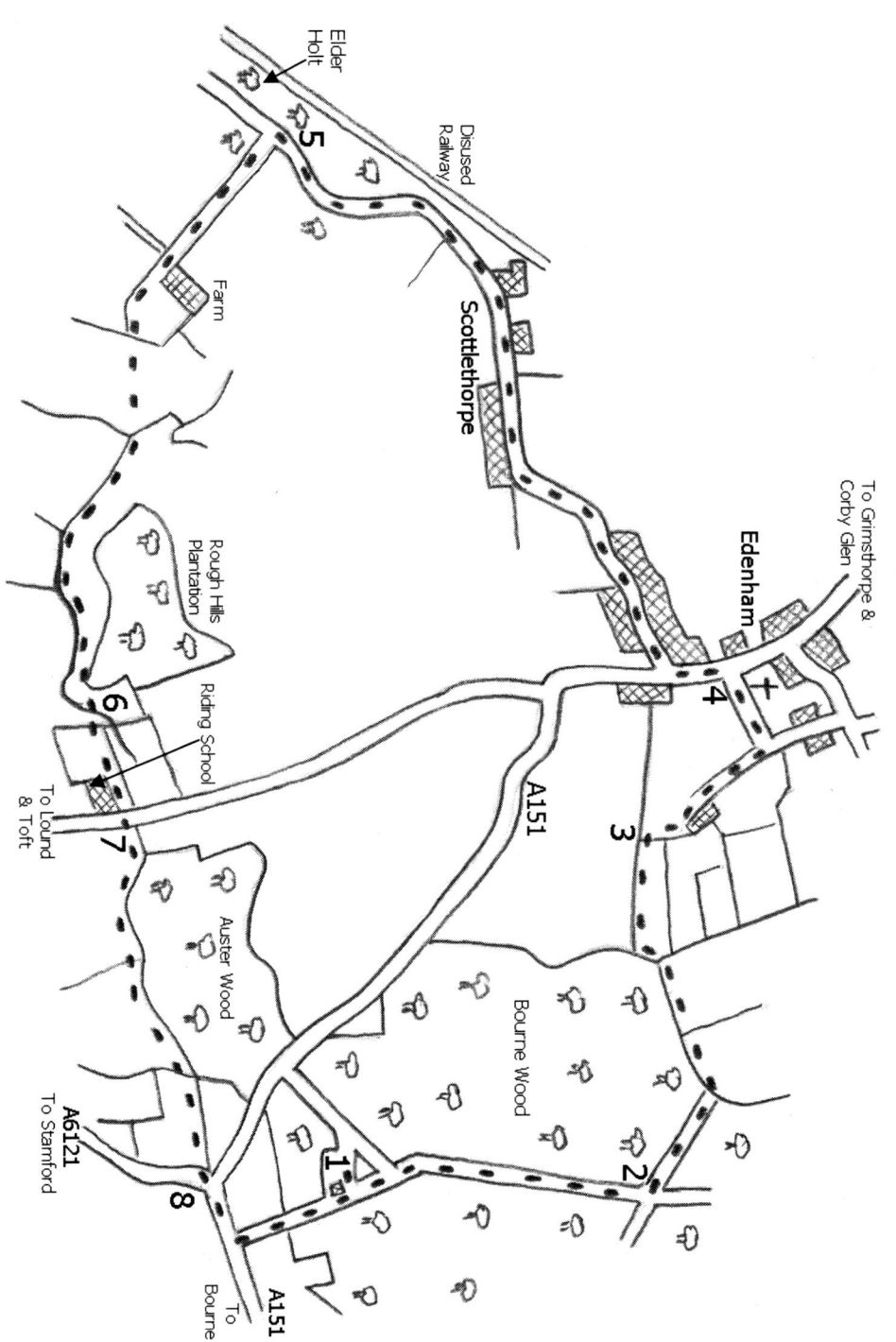

Completion of **6 Elder Holt from the previous Page**

7   Go over the road and keep direction with Auster Wood on the left. Step over the stile 70yds from the corner and continue ahead on the right hand field edge. Cross the stile at the bottom of the slope to the junction of the A151 and the A6121.

8   Follow the roadside path ahead towards Bourne, after 300yds turn left through a kissing gate at a signpost. Follow the enclosed path into Bourne Wood and keep direction to the playground, turn left into the car park to find your vehicle.

7   Fox Wood

$4^3/_4$ Miles $2^1/_4$ Hours

Find a Parking space in Morton, pubs and shops in village. No toilets. Start from the church.

1   Walk 70yds back towards the A15 and turn left at the signpost opposite the phone box. Go through the farmyard and cross the stile at the end. Bear left over the field to the top left corner. Cross the stile and take a left hand diagonal over the next field, this and other fields on this walk may be under cultivation but tracks should be visible within any crops. Bear right over the footbridge and go straight over the field ahead, another footbridge and part of the next field to a marker post standing on its own.

2   Bear left to a marker post on the edge of Dyke village, turn right through the hedge gap and follow the track down to the road. Turn right and walk along the roadside path to the A15.

3   Cross this busy road carefully and keep direction on the left hand field edge with the hedge to the left. Continue over the footbridge/stile and bear right across the field to a marker post; follow the arrowed direction over this field to a hedge gap.

4   Carry on ahead over the farm track past the signpost for Edenham along the byway, Wood Lane. Continue with the wood to the left through the gate into Bourne Woods to a more substantial hardcore forest road and turn right.

5   In a hardcore surfaced clearing, fork right through Fox Wood (part of Bourne Woods). As the trees end go past the barrier to the hardcore road, turn left and walk up to the signpost.

6   Turn right over the field corner; cross the footbridge and keep direction across the next field. Bear right over this footbridge and maintain direction over footbridges, fields and stiles; past the backs of the houses and down a fenced path to the A15 at Morton.

29:D

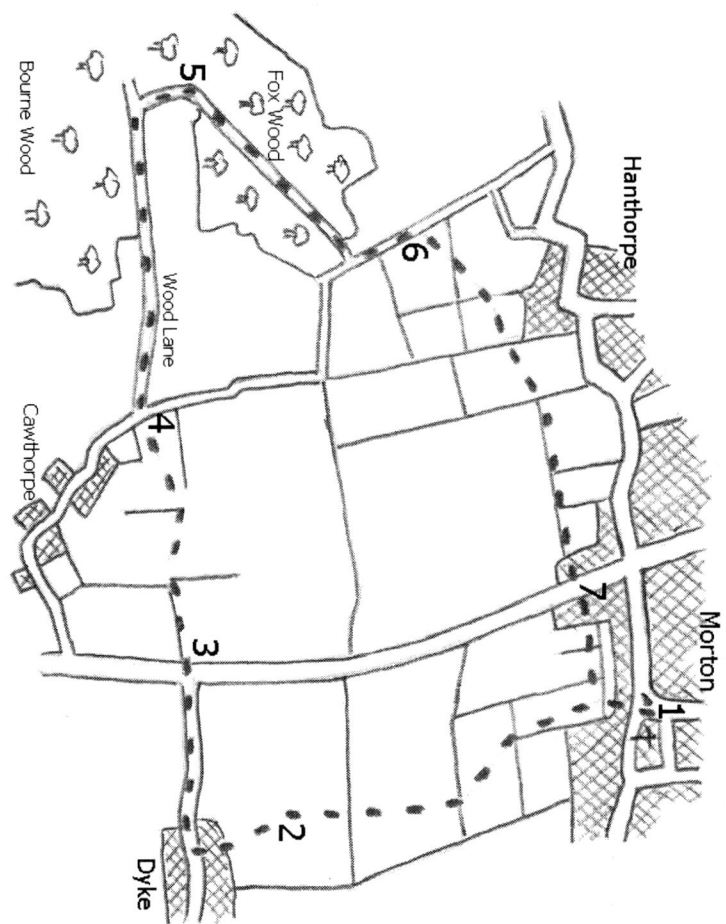

7   Cross carefully and continue ahead along Ford Lane, cross the stile at the end and go through the gate ahead. Maintain direction with the fence to the left to the cluster of five signs on a post passed on the outward route. Turn left over the stile through the farmyard back into the village to find your vehicle.

It should be easy to spot the red plumaged crossbill in Bourne Wood, but it remains surprisingly elusive. It feeds on the seeds of evergreen trees having first broken open the cone with its specially adapted bill. The spruce is a particular favourite as no other bird eats this seed.

29:D

8 Gorse Hill

6³/₄ Miles   3¹/₄ Hours

Park in the lay-by off the B1176 on the corner south of Creeton.
No toilets. No facilities.

1 Take the road from the corner signposted Counthorpe and follow the road left
under the railway. Turn right at the signpost along the drive through Elmtree Farm
and continue on the track parallel to the railway. Turn left on the right hand track
with the trees and the dyke to the left.

2 As the road turns left at the signpost go straight on over the field ahead, this
and other fields on this walk may be under cultivation paths however should be well
marked within any crop. Cross the footbridge in the dip and take a left hand
diagonal to the yellow top post left of the trees; step over the stile and across the
field to the stile at the top left.

3 Go over this stile and turn right, continue through the gate next to the cattle
grid, past the house and over two more stiles. Bear right and walk between the
lines of trees to the railway and go under the bridge, continue along the farm track
with the hedge to the right to the T-junction of tracks.

4 Turn right along the bridleway called The Drift, at the top of the rise with the
trees of Gorse Hill to the left, turn left; carry on ahead over the stile and cross the
footbridge over the West Glen River. Bear left to the marker post and turn right
uphill, step over the stile in the top corner and turn right along the right hand field
edge. Cross the stile and bear right, go through the metal gate and follow the track
left to the road in Swinstead village.

5 Turn right and walk up to the T-junction, take the road right along the B1176
towards Creeton. Continue for three quarters of a mile to the signpost at Creeton
Farm and turn right over the footbridge.

6 Go down the left hand field edge, cross through the wide gap and turn right to
carry on with the hedge now to the right. Follow the track away from the farm and
bear left to the trees. At the marker post at the crossroads of paths turn left along
the wide path with the trees to the right. Turn right at the corner and go down the
slope. Cross the stile at the marker post at the bottom and cross the footbridge
back over the river.

7 Bear left to the opposite field edge, go up to the gateway and turn right. Walk
up the slope of the right hand field edge back to The Drift and turn left, the
bridleway leads back to the outward route at the corner. Carry on down the road
ahead to the lay-by and your vehicle.

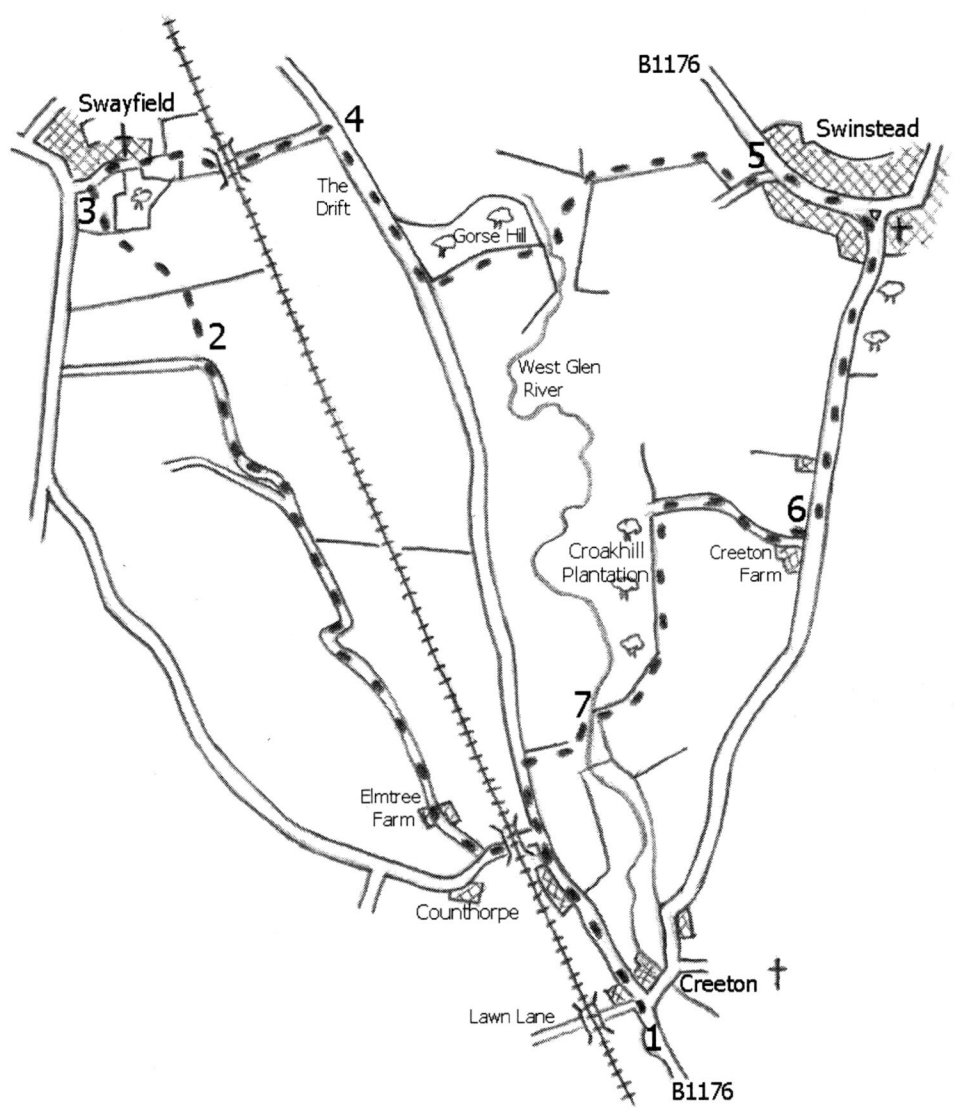

The Main East Coast railway line between Little Bytham and Carlby was the scene on July 3rd 1938 of the still unbeaten world speed record for steam locomotives. The Gresley Pacific 'Mallard', then only three months old, hauled a six coach special train peaking at the speed of 126mph for a short distance during a very high speed run. In all the publicity after the event the fact that 'Mallard' had to be taken off the train at Peterborough because of a badly damaged big end was forgotten about.

9 Callan's Lane Wood

4¼ Miles   2 Hours

Park at Callan's Lane Wood east of Kirkby Underwood just off the A15; 5 miles north of Bourne. No facilities.

1   Turn right along the road to the signpost on the left, climb over the stile and take a left hand diagonal, right of the aerials to the left hand corner of Grange Wood. These fields and others during this walk may be under cultivation but paths should be well marked through any crops.

2   Go past the signpost, cross the tarmac road and continue straight on along the farm track between fields past the telegraph pole. Pass by the trees and turn right then left, bear right into the farmyard, left past the silo and over the stile.

3   Turn left along the road away from Hawthorpe; at the signpost on the bend follow the arrowed direction over the field (a track should be visible) up to the marker post towards the left hand end of the trees. Bear left at the trees, walk up to the marker post and turn left to the twin telegraph poles.

4   Go to the right between the edge of the field and the dyke, maintain direction past the line of trees. At the gateway continue between the wire and the dyke into the corner. Turn right, walk up to the footbridge and cross, bear right through the gate and keeping the well trimmed hedge to the left go down the sloping lawn to the road in Bulby village. Go left along the road to the T-junction and turn left.

5   After 150yds turn right over the stile at the signpost, cross the field ahead, the track should be visible, to the middle of the jutting out corners. Continue direction with the hedge to the right and in the corner go straight on through the narrow hedge gap. Carry on along the left hand field edge and go through the wide gap at the end. Maintain direction to the stile at the edge of the wood.

6   Follow the track ahead through the wood, as the trees end turn left at the marker post. At the next marker post turn right over a footbridge, leave the wood and turn left over the boundary.

7   Bear diagonally right, keep direction over footbridges and fields to the corner of the hedge near the church. Bear right and follow the hedge round the church.

8   Go past the gates and turn left between the churchyard and the fence, with the dyke to the left. Turn right up to the road, turn left and walk along the road back to the parking area and your vehicle.

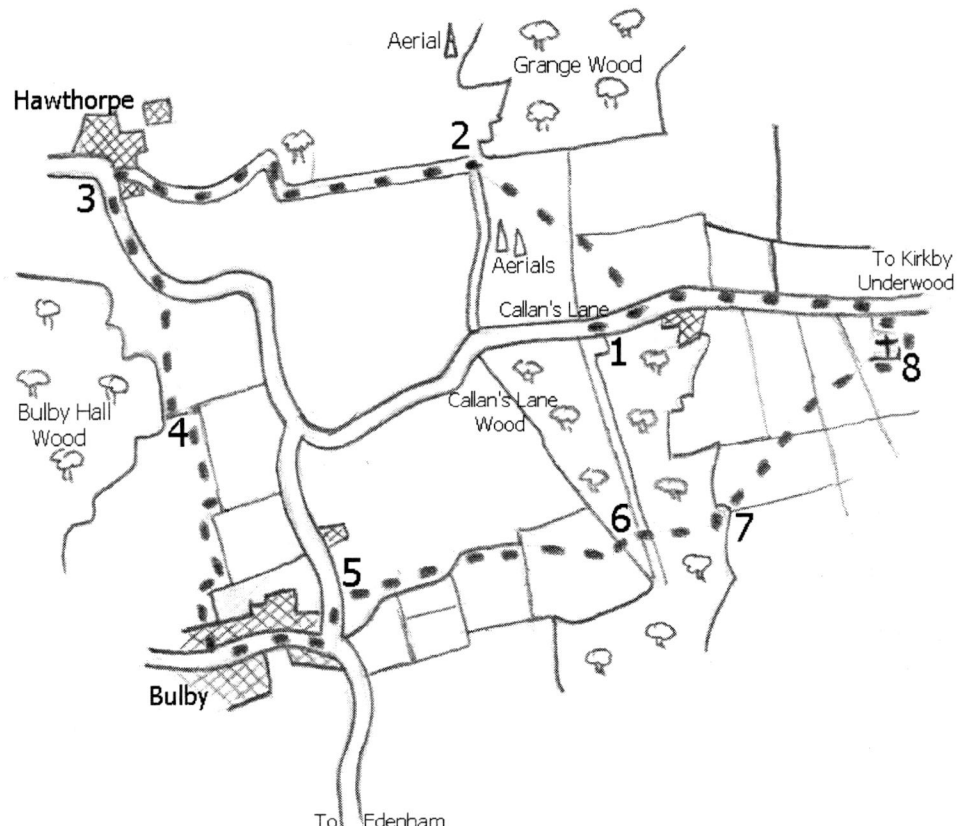

Bourne's Formula 1 heritage is reflected in the road named Graham Hill Way on the Industrial Estate as well as the memorial in the gardens between the A15 and the river, to Raymond Mays and BRM. The BRM company was founded by Mays in 1949 after his pre war experience with ERA but soon taken over by the Birmingham based Owen organisation. After a chequered history the marque won the World championship with Graham Hill in 1962. That however was the pinnacle of their success and although it produced a lot more winners the team slid down the rankings and finally closed in 1977.

The unimpressive look of Car Dyke (walk no 4) today belies its strategic importance to the Romans who built it to facilitate the transportation of food and military equipment during their 400 year occupation of England. The waterway running between Cambridge and York was constructed during a time of almost minimum technology in this country.

10   Bridgegate Lane

$4^1/_2$ Miles   2 Hours

Park in the old part of Lincoln Road in Northborough, the cul-de-sac north of the crossroads. No toilets, pub the 'Packhorse' on the old Lincoln Road in the village.

1   Walk back towards the village, straight over the crossroads and along Lincoln Road. Turn left into East Road, right into Granville Avenue and left into Church View. Go up to the railings on the right and follow the path right through the kissing gate, continue between fences right and left around the school.

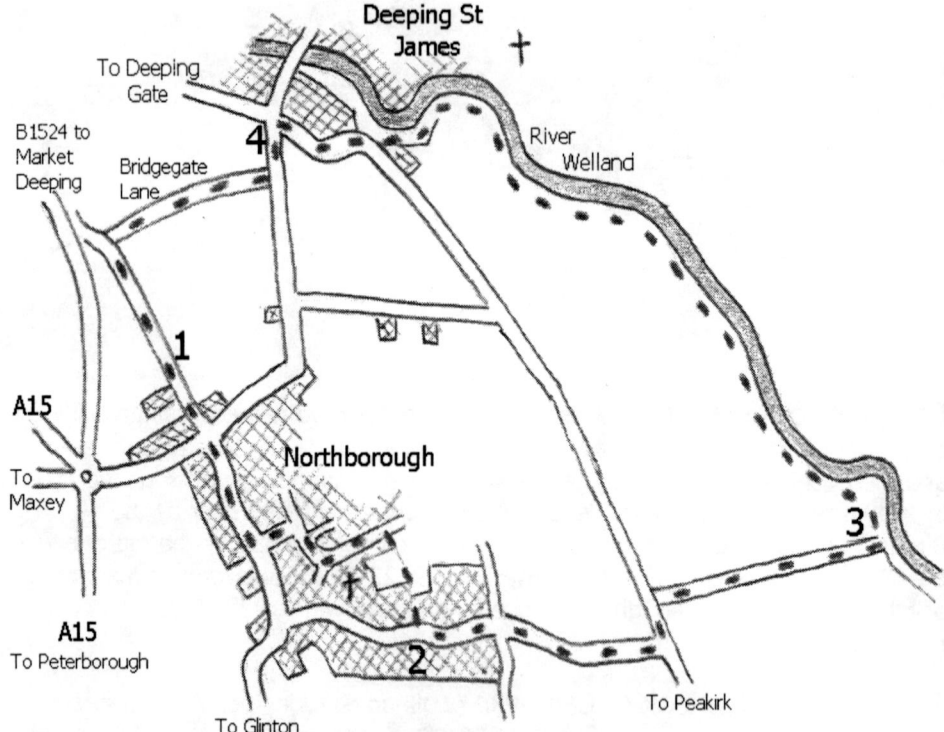

2   At the road turn left along the roadside path out of the village to the T-junction. Turn left, after 100yds turn right through the wide hedge gap and carry on along the grass drove between fields. At the end go through the gate and turn left over the stile.

3 Follow the path along the wide riverbank all the way to the kissing gate on the corner of Peakirk Road. Continue right/straight on up to the crossroads.

4 Turn left, just past the derestriction signs at a roadside seat, turn right along a hardcore farm track. Bear left with the track; at the end turn left along the disused part of the A15 to your vehicle.

Notes

Also by Clive Brown:-

'Easy Walking in South Bedfordshire and the North Chilterns'

Published by the Book Castle @ £8-99
37 walks in your favourite style

The 'Walking Close to' Series

Peterborough
The Nene near Peterborough
The Nene Valley Railway near Wansford
The Nene near Oundle
The Torpel Way (Peterborough to Stamford)
The Great North Road near Stilton

Cambridge
Grafham Water (Huntingdonshire)
The Great Ouse in Huntingdonshire
The Cam and the Granta near Cambridge
Newmarket
The Isle of Ely

Northamptonshire/Warwickshire
The Nene near Thrapston
The Nene near Wellingborough
The River Ise near Kettering
The Nene near Northampton
Pitsford Water
Rockingham Forest
Daventry and North West Northamptonshire
Rugby

Leicestershire
Rutland Water
Eye Brook near Uppingham
The Soar near Leicester
Lutterworth
The Vale of Belvoir (North Leicestershire)
Melton Mowbray
The Welland near Market Harborough

Lincolnshire
The Welland near Stamford
Bourne and the Deepings
South Lincolnshire

Suffolk
Lavenham in Suffolk
Bury St Edmunds
The Stour near Sudbury
The Orwell near Ipswich
Dedham Vale
Stowmarket
Clare, Cavendish and Haverhill
Southwold and the Suffolk Coast

Hampshire
Romsey and the Test Valley

Essex/Hertfordshire
Hertford and the Lee Valley
The Colne near Colchester
Epping Forest (North London)
Chelmsford

Wiltshire/Bath
The Avon near Bath
Bradford-on-Avon
Corsham and Box
The Avon near Chippenham

Bedfordshire/Milton Keynes
The Great Ouse near Bedford
The Great Ouse North of Milton Keynes
Woburn Abbey

Somerset & Devon
Cheddar Gorge
Glastonbury and the City of Wells
The Quantock Hills
The East Devon Coast (Sidmouth,
                              Branscombe and Beer)
Exmouth and East Devon

Norfolk
The Norfolk Broads (Northern Area)
The Norfolk Broads (Southern Area)
The Great Ouse near King's Lynn
North West Norfolk (Hunstanton and Wells)
Thetford Forest
North Norfolk (Cromer and Sheringham)

Nottinghamshire
Sherwood Forest
The Dukeries (Sherwood Forest)
The Trent near Nottingham

Oxfordshire/Berkshire
The Thames near Oxford
The Cotswolds near Witney
The Vale of White Horse
Woodstock and Blenheim Palace
Henley-on-Thames
Banbury
The River Pang (Reading/Newbury)
The Kennet near Newbury

Cumbria
Cartmel and Southern Lakeland

Hereford and Worcester
The Severn near Worcester
South West Herefordshire
                      (Hay-on-Wye and Kington)
The Malvern Hills